HOW TO UNDERSTAND YOUR CUSTOMER BEHAVIOR

I0446858

TARGETING MINDS, WINNING HEARTS FOR LASTING BRAND LOYALTY

BY

GRAY S. BERGAN

How to understand your customer behavior

Copyright

All rights reserved. No part of this publication may be distributed, or transmitted in any form or by any means, including photocopying, recording, or other electronic or mechanical methods, without the prior written permission of the publisher, except in the case of brief quotations embodied in critical reviews and certain other noncommercial uses permitted by copyright law.
Copyright © (Gray S. Bergan), (2023).

Disclaimer

The information contained in this book is for general informational purposes only. While every effort has been made to ensure that the information provided is accurate and up-to-date, [Gray S. Bergan] makes no representations or warranties of any kind, express or implied, about the completeness, accuracy, reliability, suitability, or availability of the information contained in this book for any purpose. Any reliance you place on such information is therefore strictly at your own risk.

In no event will [Gray S. Bergan] be liable for any loss or damage, including without limitation, indirect or consequential loss or damage, or any loss or damage whatsoever arising from the use of this book.

How to understand your customer behavior

About The Author

Gray started small but became a big deal in business and finance. His interest in economics as a young person made him dive into learning about money and how it shapes society. Instead of settling for a regular job after doing well in school, he explored various fields to soak up knowledge. He learned about different businesses, from new startups to big financial companies. But Gray didn't just want to understand things; he wanted to change them. He believed financial knowledge should be for everyone, not just for the elite, so he became a writer, sharing what he knew with experienced business owners and people starting out. What made him special was his knack for explaining tricky money ideas in an easy way. He also saw how technology could transform banking, so he fully embraced it, pushing for new ways to mix digital tech with old-style banking to make businesses better and more efficient.

How to understand your customer behavior

Introduction: Understanding the Customer Journey

The customer journey has emerged as a key component for companies looking to successfully understand and serve their clientele in the digital era. It includes all of the touchpoints and interactions that consumers have with a brand, from the time of initial awareness to the point of ultimate purchase and beyond. A thorough examination of each step and the customer's experience at each touchpoint is necessary to comprehend this trip.

Charting Points of Contact and Customer Experience
Every point of contact a consumer has with a brand must be located and examined as part of the touchpoint mapping process. These touchpoints can include using social media, visiting websites, sending emails, interacting with customer care, and, if relevant, visiting physical stores. Businesses may learn a great deal about consumer behavior, preferences, pain areas, and satisfaction levels at every stage by mapping these touchpoints.

To map touchpoints efficiently, data must be gathered from several sources. Website analytics, for instance, can shed light on how customers behave online, but surveys and customer feedback can yield qualitative information about preferences and levels of satisfaction. The basis for improving the client experience is this mapping procedure.

An extensive touchpoint map helps with:

1. Behavior analysis: Learning how consumers move through the various phases of the purchasing process.

2. Finding Pain Points: Determining the locations where clients may have difficulties or abandonment.

3. Opportunities for Optimization: Enhancing every point of contact to guarantee a smooth and pleasurable client encounter.

Companies use this knowledge to design strategies that attempt to enhance customer happiness and loyalty over the long run by improving the customer experience.

Improving Interaction with Customers

Building connections and maintaining client loyalty require active consumer interaction. It entails engaging clients in a meaningful way and building experiences and interactions that speak to them throughout their relationship with the business.

Here are some tactics to improve client engagement:

1. Customizing experiences according to unique tastes and habits is known as personalization.

2. Maintaining a cohesive brand image via several platforms and touchpoints is known as consistent brand presence.

3. Proactive Communication: Greeting inquiries, starting conversations, and soliciting feedback.

Good customer engagement tactics include building a feeling of community, giving consumers something of value beyond transactions, and giving them a sense of being acknowledged and appreciated.

Chapter 1: Customer behavior: What Is It?

During the day, how many decisions do you make? Five, 10, 20, or one thousand...For today, what should I eat? What apparel should I wear? What kind of day do I want to have? And the list is endless. Now consider how often we buy things every day without really thinking about them. These decisions, despite their seeming insignificance, keep marketers up at night. Since we can utilize this data to better understand the decision-making processes of our customers, we can earn more money. If marketers could identify the elements that lead their target audience to choose one product over another, wouldn't that be amazing? This information has the potential to enable the SALE of anything to anybody if properly used and examined. Even if it sounds dishonest, developing marketing plans based on customer behavior is a common practice these days.

The decisions, activities, and preferences of individuals while interacting with goods or services are referred to as customer behavior. It takes into account things like loyalty, opinions, and purchasing patterns.

Numerous elements, including societal conventions, marketing initiatives, and individual preferences, can have an impact on consumer behavior.

What are the thoughts of your customer?

The considerations of your buyers are quite important. What customers think of your product or service, how they feel about it, and what they tell others about it might be the critical factor that makes or breaks your reputation. Their considerations influence their judgments and choices regarding what you have to offer; they are not just random thoughts.

Gaining insight into your clients' needs and desires can help you better understand them. It's like having a manual on how to get better and create a far better product or service. Their opinions might vary over time, so it's important to keep listening to them and picking their brains.

Furthermore, the thoughts of your consumers are not limited to them. Other people may be impacted by their concerns. Your company's reputation is influenced by what people say about it to friends and on the internet. A clear advantage is similar to concentrating on your customers' mental processes. It helps you develop, connect with them more effectively, and create a more resolute brand image.

As people make decisions, how do they feel?
When you're making decisions, you should consider your feelings, right? Yes, the situation is the same for clients! When making a purchasing decision, they consider more than just rationality; their emotions play a big role as well.

Imagine that you are observing something fresh that you are genuinely interested in. It could make you feel energized, curious, or euphoric. You will undoubtedly need to obtain it because of these positive feelings. But if you're feeling uneasy, anxious, or frustrated, such emotions could make you err or look for something else. As a result, try to understand your clients' possible emotions when you're pitching a product or service. Be careful to capitalize on those positive emotions - ardor, trust, and happiness — in your information or experiences. They are more likely to buy from you since it gives them more confidence in their decision to choose your brand.

In what ways would people buy, use, or reject your products and services?

Once your customers decide to buy from you, that's just the start of their journey. People do not just understand and go on. In due course, people may be able to discard it after using and experiencing it. First they purchase it. But then the jesting begins—they put their newfound acquisition to work! People occasionally use it, whether it's a product or a service. Wearing apparel, utilizing a gadget, dining out, having a service like a haircut, or attending a fitness class are some examples of what this may involve.

The issue at hand is that they may eventually choose to give it away or cease using it completely. When that happens, they throw it out. The method might involve giving it away, repurposing it, selling it, or throwing it away altogether.

Being aware of your customers' whole purchase, consumption, and planning process can help you provide outstanding support at every stage. Completely ensuring people enjoy and receive value out of what they bought, as well as that they are satisfied with the entire experience long after they have finished using it, is more important than simply completing a purchase.

Each of these elements has an impact on your consumer behavior. Given that consumers are powerhouses' apparent targets. It becomes even more crucial to examine the purchasing patterns of your clients and the progression of the consumer behavior process. As a result, the analysis of purchasing behavior plays a crucial role in developing marketing strategies and action plans.

Chapter 2: Cycle of Customer Behavior

Customer behavior is mentioned as an examination of individuals, groups, and organizations' findings via observing their decisions, purchases, and rejections of goods, ideas, or experiences to satisfy their needs and desires. It discusses the efforts made by the customers at the shopping mall as well as the motivations behind their actions.

Different Types of Customers

Customers can be divided into:

1. Buyer

2. Extreme Buyer

3. Purchaser

4. Institutional Purchaser

Analysis of Consumer Behavior

It is significant for the cycle of buyers and customers and the purchasing process, which supply most of the commercial center. Once the market has been thoroughly examined,You are able to understand the things that are in demand across the commercial center, which ones have expired, and how to present the item to a consumer. Currently, we may agree that buyers play the role of performers behind the scenes while focusing on buyer behavior.

A few demonstrations are played. Many tasks, such as data providers from clients to payers and disposers. Most of these roles are performed during the dynamic. However, the various use circumstances of these vocations made them distinct.

For instance, a father could take on the character of a force to be reckoned with while his child is involved in the shopping process, but he can also play the part of the person who discards the products after his family members have used them.

Type of Customer Behavior

1. Complex purchasing behavior – When a customer purchases an expensive and fascinating object, the mind-boggling purchasing behavior approach is refined. They have now done a great deal of research

in light of purchasers who are really interested in the procurement process before efficient money management. examples include purchasing a bicycle, a home, etc.

2. Discord: decreasing purchasing behavior When consumers behave in this way, it seems as though they are confused for brands among themselves and others. However, they are significantly more focused on the procurement process. These situations usually arise when a client receives a follow-up evaluation or acknowledges that she may regret her decision after a brief

3. Consistent purchase behavior - This type of behavior is explained by the fact that consumers are not as committed to the brand or item's category. For instance: You went to the market to buy bread. You may get the sort of bread you're looking for there. In this case, you are more concerned with the bread itself than the brand it is made of. Put simply, it might mean

that you are following a traditional example but aren't a fan of any one brand.

different ways of searching for behavior In this type of customer behavior, customers typically look for a few assortments. Every time they make a purchase, they choose different things.

Factors Influencing the Behavior of consumers

The five categories of traits that buyers use to guide their processes.

Specific Variables:

Three important individual factors are included in this calculation:

1. Orientation: In addition to this, customers' purchasing behaviors also vary based on their orientation. A man and a woman can communicate two different kinds of judgments, as is often the case. Moreover, different needs drive people to make different choices.

2. Pay - Pay also plays a significant role in shifting consumers' inclinations from one brand of product to another. A person with more income often chooses the most opulent things that he can afford; in any event, a person with lower income will choose less costly goods. Additionally, in some circumstances, those with ample funds may choose to spend on a luxurious lifestyle and entertainment while others with lower salaries will avoid it. Poor people will never be able to meet their basic needs for clothing, food, and shelter, whereas wealthy people will always choose the opulent.

3. Education –Education is one of the perspectives that may change the world. Should someone receive instruction, they may be able to do better study before sending their patient closer than someone who has not had any training.

Age and Life Cycle Factors
Growing older coincides with changes in consumer purchasing behavior. People develop, and with them,

certain needs. Diapers and baby bottles, for example, are designed for little children and are not intended for use by adults.

Cultural Aspects

The following cultural elements are imposed on the process of consumer behavior:

Culture

Culture is a belief system that can be trusted, and it's also a perspective that people pick up early on from their own familial backgrounds. We are divided by this culture in a variety of ways, including via cuisine, customs, attire, and conduct. Additionally, various nations and cultures may have diverse perspectives on this culture.

Subculture

Subcultural divisions such as caste, class, and gender occur within later cultures. As an example, Hindu females marrying in red attire, while Christians married in white, represents the distinct beliefs and perspectives of each caste.

Societal class

Social class is the division of society according to its financial status, social standing, and level of achievement in the economy. Based on their educational background and line of work, these classes are categorized. When individuals make decisions, buy things, and consume things, they also communicate differently depending on their social status, which has an impact on consumer behavior.

Factors related to society

This social component depends on the relationships that individuals or groups of individuals have with one another—via blood, marriage, adoption, or continued living together. Families have a significant impact on the Consumer Behaviour Process because individual characteristics shape a person's personality, beliefs, perceptions, and tastes.

Family

When a person or group of individuals are connected to one another via marriage, blood, adoption, or cohabitation, they are referred to as family. A family has a significant impact on consumer behavior as well since members of the same species tend to rotate their views, personalities, mental processes, and tastes in accordance with their family.

Reference group: People or a local group of people who look to anybody for advice while making a purchase are considered members of this reference group. A person's beliefs, judgments, behavior, and values are often influenced by the group of references, hence this kind of reference collection might have an impact on the Purchaser Conduct Cycle. similar to friends, neighbors, and teachers.

Employment and Status: An individual's employment is considered to be based on their status, which is determined by a certain group. Most of the time, people choose what they buy depending on their specific employment and standing in society. They decide what to buy based on what seems like a status in their group. Advertisers so typically arranged and produced their products according to the primary interest group of their target audience.

Here are few factors that include:

Learning is the phrase used to describe the customer holding onto their critique of the product after using it. It may be favorable or unfavorable. Inspiration is an internal force that remains within a person and motivates them to look for anything again.

Mentality and convictions: Sometimes consumers connect with an item or have faith in it for an extended period of time. Furthermore, conviction in this context refers to a customer's special mindset about a certain product.

Mental components

Without a doubt, it is an additional factor that propels the Customer Conduct process. These components have a genuine and intellectual influence on the buyer. A few of them are -

Insight: The buyer interprets and comprehends your stuff through this. Basically, it relies on a few factors, such as how you heard it, saw it, and identified the brand.

How does the buyer think about the product and how may it alter their opinion? The first emotion is always the last, as you are well aware. As a result, a brand has defeated its product more readily than anybody else, but it may last longer in the minds of its customers.

Factors that influence our choices

1. The ability to purchase

The power of acquisition itself plays a crucial role in influencing how buyers behave. Before making a decision to acquire any good or service, the consumer frequently evaluates their ability to pay and also considers their financial situation. Whether your product or service is the greatest at it without having to meet your customers' expectations won't matter in the slightest. It will affect the bargains you make. In this case, the buyer conduct procedure and their purchasing power would be helpful in identifying the qualifying customers to get the best outcome.

2. Financial Situation

The state of the economy has a significant influence on how customers behave. The buyer's decision has a big impact on the market's new financial circumstances. The purchasing of buyers also becomes more prevalent as the economy grows. In other words, a downturn in the economy affects consumers' purchasing decisions, which in turn affects the state of the market as a whole.

3. Putting on Display Notification

Demonstrating efforts and notifications have a crucial role in influencing the customer's purchasing decision. By influencing consumers' purchasing decisions, they are renowned for enacting significant change throughout the many divisions of competing firms. Buyers' decisions may be influenced by persistent promotion to the point that they may choose one product over another.

4. Local area Impact

When we talk about local area influence, it becomes clear how important it is in influencing consumer behavior. In addition to coworkers, neighbors, clubs, and associations, there is an optional significant local community of people that includes relatives, close friends, classmates, and family members. This group of people should be visible and have a significant influence on the purchasing decisions of the buyer.

5. Individual choice

Buyer Conduct under the section on personal preferences Certain moral and ethical nuances, as well as preferences, dislikes, convictions, and dispositions, have an impact on cycles. Certain adventurous endeavors, such as individual attention, customer perspective, cuisine, design, individual viewpoints, and evaluations related to enjoyment and style, may be turned into enormously powerful variables. Missions, in any case, can assist you in making a lasting impression in these areas. Additionally, a buyer's final purchase is heavily influenced by the preferences of a certain client.

Chapter 3: Customer Behavior and Marketing Techniques

Successful businesses use customer behavior data as the cornerstone for their marketing strategy. They don't only use their ideas to create marketing strategies and goods. To find out what consumers want and how they want it, these firms are using information from other sources. On the basis of these conclusions, they then interact with them.

Creating a great customer experience (CX) is important for both the process and the outcome, and it plays a big role in building a devoted client base.

How Can Consumer Behavior Be Affected by Marketing?

Marketing has the power to significantly change customer behavior. Listed below are a few of the elements that make it successful.

1. The emotional reaction of the crowd

Prompting a response from customers is one of the benefits of marketing initiatives that helps them become successful. People will talk about your company more when they respond to your marketing activities. As a result, individuals are more inclined to purchase from you if they hear about your brand and goods more frequently.

2. The Business's Brand and Message

Using word connections and images is a great way to highlight your brand as an organization. This is a great example of how to include memes and trending words into your campaign if you want to target young people. You encourage your audience to connect your product to things they already find enjoyable and fashionable.

3. Recall of the Brand by the Audience

Using strong emotions like fear and nostalgia to sway consumer behavior is another important marketing tactic. As an illustration, consider how a product may influence your sentiments of brand loyalty if it is associated with particular companies, concepts, images, or songs from your youth. In a similar vein, if a marketing campaign makes you feel afraid, you can feel compelled to buy the product in an effort to feel less anxious and to defend yourself.

The significance of marketing to consumers

Because it focuses on comprehending customer requirements and aspirations and creating persuasive marketing techniques that resonate with the target audience, consumer marketing is essential to the success of every firm. Customer marketing is crucial for the following primary reasons:

1. Effective consumer marketing initiatives help businesses stand out from the competition and become recognized as leaders in their respective industries by raising brand recognition and exposure.

2. By continuously satisfying their wants and desires through successful consumer marketing campaigns,

businesses may cultivate long-term connections and client loyalty with their target demographic.

3. By interacting with customers through focused marketing initiatives, businesses may boost sales and income, which will contribute to their long-term success and expansion. Understanding their audience, developing successful marketing strategies, and achieving long-term success and growth are all made possible by customer marketing for organizations.

Suggested tactics for consumer marketing that work:

1. Take into account the five fundamental demands of the client. If you want to know what your customers want and how your goods and services might benefit them, this will be quite beneficial. The product, the pricing, the location, the marketing, and the people are the five basic demands of consumers. The "five Ps" refers to these five elements of the customer service procedure.

2. Use social media to hear them out.

Constantly monitor social media to find out what people are saying about your brand. While we don't advocate following people about, you should pay attention to how and when they use your items, as well as how they rate and utilize them. Customers are, after all, the most crucial component of consumer marketing. Learn how to use customer marketing to personalize your marketing efforts.

3. Make questionnaires

Another way to communicate with customers is through surveys. Making surveys will increase your revenue and reveal the strengths and weaknesses of your marketing strategy. Making errors is a necessary part of doing anything great, after all.

4. Manage the interaction with the material

Content engagement is the most crucial aspect of consumer marketing as it is built on content. You may gain greater insight into how consumers react to your marketing tactics by monitoring how they engage with your content. Planning better content is the next step to increasing your engagement rates after you have an understanding of how people interact with you.

5. Ensure your material is current.

To stay ahead of the game, it is important to keep your data up to date. To maintain the accuracy and use of the information provided, it is crucial to maintain material up to date. People dislike brands whose material on websites or social media is out of date. Here's where innovative marketing concepts shine!

To keep material current, it's critical to frequently evaluate and update information as required, search for outdated or broken links, and stay abreast of industry trends and best practices. In order to make sure the material fulfills the requirements and expectations of the audience, it's also critical to engage with them and solicit their input.

Principles of Marketing Psychology that Impact Consumer Behavior

It stands to reason that psychology influences consumer decisions whether or not we are aware of it. Consequently, marketers may strategically employ psychology to influence the decisions they desire.

1. Color Psychology: Marketing and branding efforts heavily rely on color psychology.

Our actions and decisions are influenced by color. Different hues evoke different feelings or ideas in our minds. For example, orange might inspire us to feel successful, creative, and enthusiastic, while red is typically associated with power, energy, or passion.

It's crucial to remember, though, that our perception of color is influenced by environment, culture, and personal experiences. Therefore, when deciding which colors to employ, be sure to take into account the context of your marketing campaign as well as the demography of your target audience.

2. Mutual Exchange

The notion of reciprocity stems from the human need to give something back when we get something.

In "real life" as much as in business-customer connections, reciprocity fosters stronger bonds between us. Your leads or clients will be more inclined to take action to support your business when you provide them with something of value.

3. Concentrating Impact

The concentrating effect describes how people decide. When we make decisions, our minds concentrate on a small number of elements. We tend to focus on the most notable or striking information that is stored in our memory, even when we are aware of a wealth of relevant information that may aid in our decision-making. We also frequently depend on the initial piece of information we are given.

What does this entail for you as a marketer? The goal is to focus the attention of your customers where you want them to look the most. To convince customers that a product would improve their lives, marketers should frequently pick out a few salient qualities of a product and emphasize them.

The feature or selling point that best represents your product should be very visible and the first thing potential buyers see or hear once you've determined what it is.

4. Confirmation by Social

According to the psychology theory of social proof, we use other people's behaviors and acts as guidance to choose our own actions. Ever wishing you were more like a celebrity and bought a product they endorsed? We've all been there, so don't feel bad. If that's the case, social proof has tricked you.

Social proof and reviews work so well because of social evidence. A website's conversion rate rises by 34% when testimonials are added. Additionally, consumers increasingly anticipate brand recommendations and evaluations.

How is social proof obtained? Social proof can take many different forms, such as acquiring an official certification from an authority figure or group, consumer feedback, or the endorsement of a product by an industry expert. Consider incorporating influencer marketing into your marketing plan or requesting testimonials from your present clientele.

After obtaining social proof, spread the word about it by posting testimonials on your website or reposting endorsements from influencers or celebrities on social media.

5. Insufficient supply

In accordance with the concept of scarcity, individuals value scarcer goods more highly than abundant ones. We desire something even more when there's a possibility we might not be able to have it. You may force individuals to act right away by using scarcity to drive them to make a decision.

Utilizing terms like "limited edition" or just "rare," you may occasionally employ scarcity and rarity.

Think of "limited time offer" or "temporary discount" as examples of urgent scarcity. Furthermore, exclusive scarcity occurs when a restricted quantity of individuals may buy the goods (often, this entails raising the price).

6. Power

The ability to command or shape behavior, opinion, or cognition is known as authority. When someone's background, credentials, and/or reputation make us feel confident in them, that is when we consider them to be authoritative. It also makes us feel at ease employing them.

Creating how-to material, organizing events, producing and disseminating original industry research, and presenting webinars or online courses are all effective ways to establish your brand's authority.

To put it briefly, the easiest and most efficient way to establish trust is to continually provide high-quality, informative content that speaks to the problems that your target audience is facing.

7. Innovation

Nostalgia has a straightforward concept: things labeled as "new" tend to attract more consumer interest. The newest and best things excite us because we are curious about things that are unfamiliar and new. The introduction of new items can improve our quality of life or give us a sense of social accomplishment.

8. Playfulness

One type of psychological marketing that works well is humor, which fosters goodwill and favorable associations with your company. You and your goods will stick in the minds of customers if you tell a well-written joke. Hilarious advertising has a higher recall rate among consumers—more than half do.

However, it can be more difficult than you might imagine to use comedy sensibly, responsibly, and accurately. It is imperative that you conduct thorough investigation before posting a sardonic joke or foolish remark.

Even though you can't win over everyone, you should try your hardest to make sure that no one is offended and that no one will take your joke the wrong way. Additionally, whatever comedy you use should consider your intended audience.

9. Fitts' Law

According to Fitts' Law, an individual's decision-making time is influenced by two factors: the object's size and their distance from it.

Selecting a huge object at your starting point or a group of similar objects close together takes the least amount of time. Selecting little things that are farther distant from your starting point or related objects that are far apart takes the longest.

Applications of this prediction model to human-computer interaction are common. To make your webpage or other visual design as user-friendly as feasible, you may also apply this law to UX design. For example, you should have a prominent and easily clickable CTA button.

For online buyers, who are 88% unlikely to visit a website again after a negative encounter, providing a positive user experience is essential. It's also essential for increasing your sales.

10. Using an anchor
Our subconscious decision-making process frequently uses anchors while we're weighing two or more possibilities. Intentionally or inadvertently exposed to certain bits of information constitute anchors. They turn into points of comparison that we utilize. You may carefully provide the facts you want them to know in

your marketing so they will make the choice you want them to make by employing anchoring.

Showing a product's initial price might serve as an anchor when attempting to make a sale on your website. Write the sale price next to it after that. Customers will then start using the initial price as their reference point and conclude that they are receiving a really excellent bargain as a result.

11. Oneness

The idea of togetherness appeals to people's natural need to fit in and feel like they belong. Consider the many classifications you employ to describe yourself. It's possible that you are an Asian-American mother working in marketing. You may identify more with one political or religious group than another, take pride in having graduated from a certain university, or you may just group yourself according to the interests and pursuits you find most fulfilling. You have a sense of connection with other people who belong to the groups that you identify with. With common identities, that's when unity enters the picture. One way to achieve marketing unity is to use well-written text to gently invite visitors to subscribe to your email list. Smile invites users to subscribe to the blog and become part of a community of over 30,000 forward-thinking businesses. Alternatively, you might design a whole campaign around the notion of building a community and persuading people to become members.

12. Just Envision

Assist your buyers in seeing the potential uses for your product. The secret to applying this marketing psychology idea is to consider the kind of lifestyle that your target market aspires to. Next, provide material that illustrates how using your product will lead to living the life of your dreams.

13. New Beginnings

Nothing makes us happier than a brand-new beginning. Your task is to persuade your clients that your offering is everything they require to begin again, regardless of the date. Consider promoting a campaign around a new month, new week, or even a new season (whether it be a sports season, a year-end celebration, or a personal season). Perhaps use occasions like birthdays to persuade them that this is the ideal moment to start again. You can construct practically whatever you want out of temporal landmarks—important moments in history that clearly distinguish the present from the past.

Chapter 4: What's a model of consumer behavior?

Similar to a map, consumer behavior models aid in our understanding of the motivations behind consumer purchases. It is a streamlined perspective on the decision-making process of customers. Consider it a guide to understanding consumer preferences for different products.

These buying behavior models illustrate the processes a person takes to make a purchase. They frequently involve actions including realizing a need, gathering data, weighing possibilities, and ultimately coming to a conclusion. Companies can follow the map to observe how clients make decisions, which makes these models very helpful. This aids companies in producing higher-quality goods, determining appropriate pricing, crafting impactful advertisements, and selecting retail locations. A buyer behavior model, which is very helpful for businesses, is in essence, a guide that illustrates how consumers make purchasing decisions.

various models of consumer behavior

There are, of course, many different kinds of consumer behavior models, and each one presents a unique angle on the process and motivations behind consumer decision-making. Typical consumer behavior model types include the following:

1. Customary model of consumer behavior

As a guide, the learning model shows how to make decisions throughout a shopping trip. It is all about how you absorb information and form decisions in response to your experiences. Consider it this way: you recall products that create positive memories for you, such as delicious ice cream flavors.

You might choose the same taste the next time you buy ice cream since you now know it's good. These consumer behavior models assist us in realizing the significant influence that our prior experiences have on the things we choose to buy. It's similar to how your shopping memory aids in selecting your preferences!

2. Economic model

Economic models function as your compass in the confusing world of decision-making, much like a reliable salesperson assisting you in navigating the many options in an aisle. Imagine entering a store knowing exactly what you want to get out of your financial investment. In order to do this, you don't just choose any product; instead, you carefully consider its features, cost, and compatibility with your spending limit. Your base is quality. You look for things that are functional, long-lasting, or meet any other important requirements. But excellence on its own is insufficient. Cost takes center stage. Here's where an economic model comes in, enabling you to carefully assess if the cost is appropriate for the quality provided. It's about making sure your sense of worth and the amount you're prepared to pay fit together.

The point when price and quality meet your budget is next. This trio influences how you make decisions. This precise balance is made easier with the help of an economic model, which guarantees that the product you select fits both your budget and your quality requirements.

However, it doesn't end there. Your friends in the pursuit of maximum utility—a fancy name for the joy or contentment gained from a purchase—are economic models. They serve as your guides while you search for a product that brings you long-lasting satisfaction rather than simply a brief burst of happiness. They take into account both the long-term worth and the instant enjoyment that the purchase provides.

Consider these models as your knowledgeable counselors; while they cannot foretell the future, they do offer a methodical framework for weighing your alternatives. They provide you with the means to evaluate advantages and disadvantages and compare and contrast options, so that your choices are supported by reason rather than hunches.

Economic models ultimately provide you the ability to make wise decisions. They make sure every dollar you put in, will return the maximum amount of value. They aren't magic wands; instead, they are useful instruments that take the economics of your decisions into account. This allows you to design a life in which your purchases are in line with your needs and your budget. They hold the key to maximizing your satisfaction while staying within your financial constraints.

3. Psychoanalysis modeling

In an attempt to comprehend how these subconscious feelings and ideas affect our purchasing behaviors, the psychoanalytic model delves deeply into the shadowy corners of our minds. Imagine it as if you had a tiny investigator in your mind who is constantly trying to figure out why you are drawn to particular things without you even recognizing it. This model proposes that our thoughts are operating in strange ways while we go shopping. Our decisions are shaped not only by what appears sensible or practical, but also by deeply ingrained feelings, memories, and experiences. Though we may believe we are making simple choices, a myriad of unspoken factors influence what ultimately ends up in our shopping cart. This type of thinking also suggests that marketers and businesses may utilize our unconscious wants to shape our purchasing decisions. To make their products more enticing, they craft advertisements and marketing tactics that appeal to both our rational and emotional sides.

Essentially, the psychoanalytic model reveals to us that our minds are like hidden treasure troves, with a plethora of emotions and causes influencing our purchasing decisions. It serves as a reminder that there are many hidden variables that influence our purchasing decisions, making it harder than it first appears to decide what to buy. We may become more conscious of the reasons behind our attraction to particular things by comprehending this paradigm. It's as if it sheds light on the shadowy corners of our brains, enabling us to see how decisions are frequently influenced by factors other than what first greets the sight. By becoming cognizant of these subconscious effects, we may become more educated decision-makers and conscious shoppers who understand the underlying motivations behind our choices.

4. Sociocultural Models:

Consumer behavior is modeled socioculturally, emphasizing how our environment and the society we belong to shape our purchasing decisions. Comparable to piecing together a jigsaw, where each piece symbolizes the various facets of our social milieu that influence our purchasing choices. Think of yourself as a sponge that takes up the tastes and ideas of those around you, including your family, friends, and the culture in which you live. These imply that the beliefs of our friends and family, as well as the traditions and conventions we uphold, have a big influence on the things we decide to buy. Sometimes we choose a product because it fits with what we've learned from people in our community or because, after consulting them, it seems like a wise decision.

These models essentially illustrate how our immediate environment influences the way we purchase.

In essence, there is more to our buying choices than just personal taste. The customs, principles, and mutual convictions of our social networks and the larger cultural milieu in which we live have a significant impact on them.

Recognizing the affects of our social networks and cultural background, together with our own tastes, all combine to shape our purchasing patterns.

5. The Black Box model

The Black Box concept is a fantastic approach to understand how your selections about what to buy come together, like some sort of mysterious container full of components that are essential to knowing how customers behave. It may be compared to a mystical box that has inputs, processes, and outputs that all work invisibly, like a mysterious puzzle that has to be solved.

The fundamental components of it are the inputs, or the stimuli that cause you to make decisions. They may be recommendations, ads, or product displays; they could even be like the jigsaw pieces that are provided to you when you're shopping. They are the first indicators that catch your attention and make you want to learn more.

But what's really going on within this mysterious black box is hidden from view. This is the point of magical activity. Your brain painstakingly goes over the information it receives, processing it all like a secret laboratory inside your head. Think of it as an amalgam, a combination of ideas, impressions, and assessments, all masked from public view.

Here, your unique experiences, opinions, and preferences are combined with the information you have been given by the unseen cognitive gears. As if there were some kind of complex alchemy at work, turning the outside stimuli into a customized decision-making procedure.

This secret cerebral activity culminates in the output, which is the ultimate choice or course of action. That is the result of this enigmatic process taking on inside the black box. The outcome of the complex interaction between the outside stimuli and your internal cognitive processes may be a decision to buy, not to buy, or to make no purchase at all.

The intricacy of our mental processes throughout the purchasing process is shown by this Black Box model. It illustrates how, despite the multitude of inputs we are subjected to, a large portion of our decision-making takes place in the hidden domains of our mind, outside of our conscious awareness.

Chapter 5: The Process of Consumer Decision Making

Consumer decision-making is a multi-step, intricate process that includes searching, weighing options, making a purchasing choice, and evaluating the experience after the purchase. Customers base their purchasing decisions on a variety of elements, such as past encounters, outside cues, and unique purchasing habits. Because they have a strong emotional bond with a company and have had favorable experiences, loyal customers are more inclined to make repeat purchases.

Before making a purchasing choice, buyers weigh a variety of internal impulses and criteria, including price, quality, and brand reputation, while considering alternative items. In order to ascertain if the goods or service fulfilled their expectations and whether they are happy with their purchase, post-buy assessment is also essential.

To effectively attract and keep customers, businesses must comprehend the decision-making process of consumers and develop marketing tactics that cater to each stage of the buyers' journey. Businesses may foster strong client connections and raise the likelihood that consumers will stick with them by offering high-quality goods and services.

1. Problem Identification

The first step is figuring out exactly what the consumer wants. The customer feels that something is lacking and has to be fixed in order for them to feel normal again. If you can determine the exact time your target audience develops these needs or wants, it would be fantastic to promote them.

2. Information collection.

This is the search step of the process. One that is always changing, moving from window shopping to Google, the new storefront (other search engines appear to be available, apparently).

People provide information not only about products and services but also via recommendations. At this stage, a customer is beginning to think about risk management. A buyer may make a list of advantages and disadvantages to help them make a selection. Given that individuals usually don't want to second-guess their decisions, it could be beneficial to invest extra time on risk management.

3-Examining the Available Options

Here is where people start to ask questions. Is this really the greatest project for me to work on? Does a different product have to be used? In the case that the answers are unfavorable or suggest that an alternative product is needed.

The customer will begin searching for the greatest deal once they've determined what will satisfy their requirement or demand. according to the factors that are important to them, whether it be quality, cost, or something else. Once they have read many reviews and compared prices, consumers ultimately select the product that best suits the majority of their needs.

4- purchase

Now, the consumer has made a decision on what to buy and where to buy it based on the information acquired.

By now, the consumer has either considered all the available information and reached a rational choice, chosen based on personal ties or past experiences, or given in to sales or marketing efforts. More often, a mix of all these factors has led to the customer's decision.

5 – Satisfaction or unhappiness after buying

The evaluation stage is critical for the client and the business. Were the claims made about the goods in the marketing and advertising efforts true? Were expectations met or exceeded by the product?

In stage 2 of their next customer journey, a client who finds that the product lives up to their expectations and fulfills the promises given to them might become a brand ambassador and encourage other potential consumers to buy your product, therefore increasing the chance that they would buy it from you again. This also holds true for negative reviews, which, if they surface during stage 2, may lead a potential customer away from your products.

The Impact of Feelings on Consumer Choices

Because they affect how a person views a product or service, emotions play a critical role in consumer decision making. It is more likely for consumers to base their choice to buy a product or brand on their perceptions of it than just its attributes or cost.

Consumers and companies may form a deep link via positive feelings like enjoyment, enthusiasm, and trust, which can result in repeat business and loyalty. Negative feelings, on the other hand, such rage or disappointment, can turn customers against a company.

Businesses must comprehend how emotions play a part in customer decision-making in order to develop marketing tactics that resonate with their target market.

What influence can you have on the process of making decisions?

You have the chance to have a significant influence on your customer during the decision-making process. You may maximize your newfound comprehension of the decision-making process of consumers by utilizing the marketing tools that Constant Contact provides. They consist of:

1. Ads: You need to show up in your customers' first solution searches when they start their trip. Use SEO, social media marketing, and Google marketing to make sure key members of your specialized demographic can see you.

2. Branded email templates: Think about the aspects of your brand that resonate best with your target audience. Enhance this identity, and make it simple to

produce professional and consistent contact by using Constant Contact's branded templates.

3. Automated emails: These can help you reach out to and convince hesitant clients, particularly in the research stage or when there is an abandoned cart during the buying stage. Throughout the decision-making process, reassure your customers with compelling messages and insightful material. Utilize automation to maintain customer attention during the evaluation phase.

4. Audience segmentation: This potent technique may assist you in personalizing your communications to clients who are still unsure about your brand when combined with customer data. Content may be easily customized and sent to the clients who would benefit from it the most.

5. Email tracking: You can monitor your clients' activity and engagement levels with the use of email and social media analytics. Recall that your objective

is to maintain consumers' interest in your brand after they have completed the evaluation phase.

6. Website building: With the help of this tool, you can easily design websites that have an effect and facilitate online purchasing for your consumers. Simple-to-use websites and portals can help you hold onto satisfied clients.

7. Social media engagement: Run social media campaigns to maintain the interest of devoted followers and clients in your business. Recurring business, strong word-of-mouth referrals, and reliable evaluations may all be obtained via social media.

Building a long-term connection based on trust and involvement is crucial to turning a paying client into a brand ambassador. Communicate with clients right away by using online resources at each stage of the decision-making process.

How to understand your customer behavior

Chapter 6: Division of Buyer Conduct

Differentiating between client segments and buyer types has always been essential. Strong division is now even more important as customer satisfaction and personalization play a major role in an organization's success. Selecting a division strategy that makes sense and functions for your company is essential. Most advertisers use these strategies for social division.

1. Observing what clients do while researching a product or service might provide important information about the features, benefits, applications, and challenges that most encourage them to buy it.

These are the crucially convincing arguments that influence a customer's choice to purchase when they perceive at least one benefit to be significantly more important than the others.

Similar to purchasing toothpaste, a buyer may look for one of four things: taste, value, brightness, or sensitive teeth.

2. Individual and inclusive events determine the time-sensitive/event-driven behavior parts.

3. Ratio of Utilization

The frequency with which a customer engages with or purchases a certain goods or service is another well-known tactic for conduct-based client segmentation. Exemplary behavior can serve as a powerful predictor of life satisfaction and, in turn, loyalty or commitment.

4. Brand Trustworthiness Status

Reliable clients are the most valuable resource for a business. They have the best lifetime value, need minimum maintenance, and might act as brand ambassadors.

Using social information analysis, customers may be grouped based on how devoted they are, allowing advertisers to better understand customer wants and ensure they are being satisfied.

Loyal customers should receive special treatment and benefits, such as enrollment in exclusive reward programs, in order to foster and strengthen the client connection and support future Web-based businesses.

5. User Status: A variety of user statuses are conceivable, depending on your firm. Several examples are:

1. A non-user group
2. Opportunity
3. The original purchasers
4. Regular clients
5. Defectors (previous clients who switched to a rival)
6. Stage of Client Excursion

Advertisers may divide the audience according to buyer availability, synchronizing information and personalizing interactions to improve transformation at every step. Additionally, it gives them the ability to identify the points at which customers are declining, enabling them to identify the biggest challenges and, in any case, opportunities for improvement regarding post-purchase propensities.

A further way for division in addition to these conventional approaches is the RFM model. This approach is well-liked by online business advertisers because it enables web-based companies to create customer experiences depending on the data they know about each customer class.

One behavior division model is called RFM, or Recency, Recurrence, and Financial Worth.

There are two approaches to handling the RFM model examination:

1. In a physical sense, by physically delivering your data set to a calculation sheet and breaking down your customers in accordance with the RFM examination guidelines; RFM analysis and division reveals who your most loyal and advantageous clients are in addition to:

Create ideas specifically tailored for your customers; Identify the products and brands that are hurting your online company; Address certain problems related to the customer experience.

In order to maintain the loyalty of your customers and supporters despite the might of your competitors, observe how they behave, pay attention to them, and build a rapport with them before acting only on impulse.

Identified and arranged clients' trouble spots
Specific problems that both existing and future customers of your business center encounter are known as trouble spots. They run the risk of impairing the business-customer relationship. It's challenging to become acquainted with every client's struggles, though. Therefore, implementing strategies to avoid common trouble areas in your company methods is the most wise course of action. Since leads and prospects often have no idea what concerns them, investigating difficulties is often your job.

To attract business, therefore, you should help potential customers identify their pain points and demonstrate to them how your products and services are suitable solutions.

Chapter 7: How to Affect Consumer Behavior using Psychological Pricing

Businesses employ psychological pricing as a crafty tactic to sway customer behavior without the conscious knowledge of the customers. In the retail industry, prices are deliberately chosen to capitalize on the psychological peculiarities of consumers, much like a magician's sleight of hand. By using prices like $9.99, firms avoid using simple pricing strategies like selling an item for $10. For what reason? Because our eyes pick up on the first digit we see, $9.99 appears to be a lot less expensive than $10 even if it is just one penny less. Charm pricing is when we use this to provide the impression of a better deal by manipulating our sense of worth.

Additionally, companies use strategies like package pricing, which involves combining items to give customers a sense of value for their money. Have you ever seen promotions such as "Combo Meal Deals" or "Buy 2, Get 1 Free"? Bundle pricing is in effect there. It pushes customers to see a better value proposition, persuading them to buy something they would not have otherwise thought about.

Taking use of our subconscious tendencies is the core of psychological pricing. Rather than using reason, people frequently base their purchasing decisions on feelings, whims, or perceived worth. These pricing tactics encourage people to make decisions quickly by deftly appealing to these inclinations.

Businesses must comprehend these psychological pricing strategies. It enables them to place their goods or services strategically, which eventually raises the possibility that customers will make a purchase. Understanding how customers think about costs and decide what to buy may help businesses develop pricing strategies that play on these subliminal cues, changing customer behavior and increasing revenue.

Tips for Applying Psychological Pricing:

The following Tips should be taken into account when applying psychological pricing strategies:

1. Know your audience: To effectively customize your pricing tactics, you must have a thorough understanding of the tastes and purchasing patterns of your target audience.

2. Test and evaluate: Try out various price strategies and pay careful attention to how they affect sales and consumer behavior.

3. Express value clearly: To support price and improve client perception, express the worth of your goods or services.

4. Remain competitive: To make sure your rates stay competitive in the market, keep an eye on your rivals' pricing tactics.

A strong technique that has the potential to greatly influence customer behavior and increase sales is psychological pricing. Businesses may successfully influence customer decision-making and increase their bottom line by comprehending the numerous approaches and using them wisely.

How Can the Appropriate Price Point Be Set?

Deciding on the ideal pricing point for your goods or services may have a big impact on your bottom line and client behavior. The anchoring effect is a potent psychological pricing strategy that may be used. You may sway clients' perceptions of the worth of your products and steer them into purchases that advance your company by carefully adjusting your prices.

1. Recognize the Anchoring Effect:
The propensity for people to base a significant portion of their decision-making on the first piece of information they are given is known as the "anchoring effect." This means that, when it comes to pricing, a customer's view of one price might be influenced by the price they see for the first time. Customers may perceive costs as substantially lower even though they are still objectively high if they first view an expensive item.

2. Establish a High Anchor: Consider creating a high anchor for your products or services in order to take advantage of the anchoring effect. This can be accomplished by selecting a high-end option that is initially seen as costly by customers. By doing this, you might create a standard that would be utilized to assess other, less costly options. This might make those less priced options seem more fair and tempting.

A retailer of apparel, for example, may launch a premium brand of merchandise that costs more. Even while most consumers won't buy these expensive things, having such high-end selections might affect how they see the retailer's other, more reasonably priced products. Consumers may decide to buy these less expensive products because they think they're a better value than the premium line.

3. Make Use of Decoy Pricing

The employment of decoy pricing is another efficient technique to take advantage of the anchoring effect. To do this, present a third alternative that acts as a ruse to increase the perceived value of the target option. To make the target choice seem more appealing in contrast, the decoy alternative should be deliberately priced.

Consider a software firm that has three pricing tiers, Basic, Standard, and Pro. $50 a month for the Basic plan. The Pro package is priced at $150 per month, while the Standard plan is priced at $80. The Basic plan is more likely to be chosen by clients over the other alternatives because it presents the Standard plan as a ruse, giving them the impression that it offers cheaper value.

4. Check Various Anchors:

Remember that depending on your target market and the type of items or services you offer, anchoring may or may not be beneficial. The ideal pricing points and anchors for your company must thus be determined through A/B testing. Find the best mix that optimizes consumer impression and boosts sales by experimenting with various price points, anchor alternatives, and decoy pricing techniques.

Your pricing approach may be significantly impacted by your comprehension of and use of the anchoring effect. Through the use of decoy pricing, high anchoring, and careful testing, you may sway client behavior and steer them toward purchases that will help your firm.

Taking Advantage of the Charm of Odd Numbers:

Determining a product or service's price is a strategic choice that has a big influence on how customers behave. It involves more than merely picking a number. The impact of odd numbers—especially nine—on psychological pricing is an intriguing feature.The allure of odd numbers is their capacity to convey a sense of worth and accessibility. Customers may perceive a product priced at $19.99 to be substantially less expensive than one priced at $20, for instance. This little price difference may have a big influence on what people decide to buy.

Using our innate ability to assimilate information fast and easily is one prominent reason for why strange pricing works so well. We naturally round down prices ending in 9 to the next whole number in our minds, which makes them appear more reasonable. When consumers are comparing costs or making snap judgments about what to buy, this mental shortcut can have a significant impact. It is impossible to overstate the influence odd numbers have on psychological packaging. Businesses may affect consumer behavior, boost revenue, and improve customer satisfaction by deliberately utilizing the charm of 9. To develop pricing methods that work, it is important to understand the cognitive biases that influence consumer decision-making.

Hints on utilizing the power of nine in your pricing plan:

1. Strategically use odd pricing: To convey value, think about concluding your prices with 9. For instance, you may attempt to price a product at $49.99 rather than $50.

2. Try out various odd numbers: Although 9 is the most frequent odd number, feel free to try out other odd digits as well. For example, charging $39 for a product can also have the same result.

3. Call attention to the price difference: To make a sale or discounted pricing more noticeable, call attention to the price difference. Show the $20 savings, for example, by displaying the original price as $99 and the discounted price as $79, respectively.

How to understand your customer behavior

Chapter 8: Pain point of customer

Identifying and addressing the problems that your consumers are having is a terrific approach to differentiate yourself from the competition and demonstrate your concern for them. There are three places to pay attention to when it comes to pain spots.

1. Identifying the pain spot of your client.

2. Gaining their confidence

3. Resolving their pain point

Better customer experience may be achieved by recognizing and addressing consumer pain points, and organizations place a high value on improving customer experience.

Customer pain points are certain issues that your company's clients or potential clients are facing in the marketplace. In essence, these are any issues that the client could run across during their interaction with them. Naturally, there might be a wide variety of these issues, so it might not be as simple as you first believe to identify them all. Reaching the core of your consumers' problems requires some creative problem-solving and putting yourself in their position. Even though a pain point might be a little or huge problem, it's usual to categorize pain points so you can approach solving them more effectively.

How Much Do Pain Points Matter?

Identifying pain spots in sales is crucial for salespeople. When you are aware of the customer's business pain issues, you can:

1. Determine whether or not the client is a great fit.

2. Establish a more intimate connection with clients

3. Finalize additional agreements

Rather than talking about the attributes of your goods or service, you would be solving the issues your clients are facing. In order to learn more about their issues and then offer your product or service as a remedy, you'll probably want to probe them with inquiries.

common categories of pain points:

1. Pain Points in Productivity

This category includes all of the customer's complaints about wanting a more streamlined or efficient way to interact with businesses. These clients want to maximize their time, therefore anything that complicates the purchasing process will irritate them.

By introducing features like fewer stages in the checkout process and smarter agent routing for customer assistance, you can cut down on redundancy and friction in your purchasing process. However, increasing your company's productivity does more than merely make it more appealing to potential customers. It also involves providing goods that draw clients who wish to increase their productivity. If you wish to address productivity pain points with your goods, you should concentrate on the following features:

- Productivity optimization: How can your product make your consumers' time more productive? The urge to optimize our time is something that most of us can relate to, especially in the digital era when we are only truly offline while we sleep. You'll attract potential clients if you can explain to them how your product will increase their productivity and provide them with greater concentration.

- Boost Comfort: Customers are more inclined to utilize your product if they have a favorable experience with it. Comfort might be an additional strategy to boost productivity for clients who are more vulnerable to productivity pain points.

- Convenience: Consumers frequently choose something simple and practical over something more expensive but less practical. Customer productivity issues might not be a primary concern for every company; this will vary depending on the goods and services you provide. If you provide software for personal or business usage, one of your main selling points is undoubtedly more productivity. It could be overstated to suggest that getting a new pair of shoes will increase your productivity and allow you to spend more time with your family if you are a shoe salesperson. The idea is that you shouldn't handle all client pain points equally since they are not. The services you provide to your clientele and the nature of your business will determine how equal they are.

2. Pain Points for Support

The parts of the purchasing process when your consumers aren't getting assistance are known as support pain points. When a consumer is unable to discover the solution to a critical inquiry on your website or through prompt customer care, they will look elsewhere.

3. Problems with Money

Prospective consumers who are spending excessive amounts of money on their existing suppliers or products and wish to reduce their expenditure are considered financial pain points. Simply expressed, timing issues with money are known as financial pain points for clients. Here are a few instances of financial points to consider:

- Expensive membership fees or subscription plans.
- Poor-quality items that, although being advertised as long-lasting, will need to be replaced regularly.
- Extra charges applied at the register.
- A lack of clarity on the ultimate cost.
- A sharp increase in fees following a certain amount of time.

4. Pain Points in the Process

Process pain points are instances where your company's less-than-ideal procedures are causing customers to experience friction or discomfort. In certain cases, this may be something as simple as the fact that your call center is only available for eight hours a day or that users must navigate several pages on your website in order to find the information they want. Consumers who find the purchasing procedure with your firm too complicated will move to another brand since they value ease. It's really estimated that 75% of consumers may switch brands if they find the shopping experience too challenging. But occasionally, the process pain areas might not be as apparent to you, which is why it's crucial to speak with your customer.

Which Pain Point Levels Are There?

There are several phases of pain. Being aware of the customer's level will enable you to take the appropriate action.

Level 1: Despite being dissatisfied with their current circumstances, the client is nevertheless comfortable utilizing it.

Level 2: The client feels depressed but continues to use the current product.

Level 3: The client is prepared to transfer since they are obviously dissatisfied.

Level 4: The client is prepared to move on and is looking for a replacement for the current tier.

Level 5: The client no longer believes that a solution can be found.

It is obvious that the consumer is more inclined to listen to you and choose your solution when they are in the last three phases.

How to Determine the Pain Points of Your Customers

1. Conduct in-depth market analysis

The focus of qualitative market research is on in-depth answers from clients who are given the chance to fully describe their issues. In comparison, a 1–10 scoring system or yes/no questions and responses are the main emphasis of quantitative market research. A few factors make qualitative market research preferred:

Finding pain spots is overly limited by quantitative market research. When there is limited room for interpretation, quantitative research is ideal. For instance, conducting surveys to collect consumer information for marketing purposes is frequently beneficial. How many hours a day do you spend on your phone? can be a question you have. 0–2 hours, 2-4 hours, 4-6 hours, and so on might be the responses. But there are frequently no easy answers when it comes to pain areas.

Every customer's pain point is unique. Even if you classify your pain spots, there may still be a lot of variation among the groupings. Giving the client the chance to completely describe their problem can help you determine which problems are typical, which aren't, which require serious consideration, and other factors. You must pose pertinent queries. This one is crucial and a big part of the reason quantitative market research isn't appropriate in this situation. Whether we work for a company or are its employees, we frequently find it difficult to perceive things from the viewpoint of the client. You are, after all, an expert in your field and aware of the benefits you provide to clients. On the other hand, you might not know how conscious the buyer is of that knowledge. Furthermore, it's possible that you have never even considered a pain issue that your company can fix but are completely ignorant of. This is probably not a problem that you have addressed in your customer questions if you have never thought about it. Qualitative research is particularly effective because of this. The consumer can provide as much information as they desire in response to open-ended queries. An unstructured open forum is another option you have for allowing them to share their experiences.

2. Consult with Your Sales and Customer Support Teams

Every day, your sales and customer support personnel interact with consumers on the front lines of your company. Because of this, they are excellent sources of information on the problems faced by customers. It's crucial, nevertheless, that your agents recognize the distinction between the problems they face and those of the customers. You might wish to take action if their systems aren't operating properly. Agents may receive remarks from customers that sound something like this: "I liked your product when I bought it last, but it's far too expensive without a discount, so I went with a different company this time." The alternative would be "I don't want to buy from you again because I was shocked to see extra charges added on at the checkout that I wasn't expecting." Here are examples of financial difficulties and a segment of your business that you can be losing out on significant profits from because of your client-rejecting policy.

It's also important to remember that pain spots require ongoing thought and evaluation. As customers' expectations of the market change over time, so do their pain issues. Furthermore, it would be impractical to respond to every complaint a client raises. For example, some consumers may never purchase a product beyond a particular threshold since that is how they conduct their lives. Knowing when to address a pain issue and when it wouldn't really provide value is important.

3. Examine internet testimonials

Finding client pain points is facilitated by reading reviews. Keep an eye on the comments that your clients make about your goods on social media. Elevate the experience by perusing client testimonials on top review platforms.

Peer-to-peer review platforms offer a wealth of consumer complaints, giving companies an excellent opportunity to learn about and resolve client complaints. You may even identify and take advantage and disadvantages of your brand and your rivals from the viewpoint of the client because a lot of people utilize internet review sites to share their opinions.

Qualitative research is really beneficial. After you've gathered feedback from various sources, visit community forums to uncover recommendations that can benefit your business.

4. Pay close attention to your rivals

You might not be able to reach every customer persona, no matter how hard you try. That doesn't imply, though, that you can't ever get their attention. Simply said, your brand's marketing doesn't speak to the demands of your target audience.

This is where keeping a careful eye on the brands of your competitors may be beneficial. Each company approaches addressing client pain issues in a unique way. Making an educated choice when it comes time to review and update your customer experience strategy is made easier by analyzing these pain areas.

5. Employ intent signals

When a consumer has discomfort, they first conduct basic internet research to resolve it on their own. Typically, they browse websites, peruse blogs, get materials, and leave their mark. Intent signals allow you to follow them. By doing this, you may reach out to clients early on and get an advantage over rivals.

6. Carry out keyword analysis

Knowing what people are actually searching for related to your sector on search engines will help you identify the true source of the issue. There are several methods for conducting research and determining the search terms.

The actions you can do to complete this exercise are listed below.

1. Examine the website, offers, FAQs, and feature landing pages of your competitors.

2. Make a list of the problems that customers are having that they have addressed. It's possible that you overlooked the same thing. Examine how you might use those in your brand messaging or on your website.

3. Look at their advertisements more closely by conducting a Google search for them. The greatest way to target client pain spots is via these advertising.

Examine if the copy in your advertising needs to be changed.

4. List all of the integrations that the brand of your rival has made available. How do they provide a flawless client experience? Permit connection with tools and applications that help your consumers with their buying process.

Tips for Addressing Consumer Pain Points

Upon recognizing a customer's pain problem, the next step is to devise a strategy to address it. The customer's pain issue and what your firm can provide in terms of a solution will determine how different the answer is. A "confusing and hard to navigate customer service channels," for instance, may be recognized as a customer pain issue. If they can't quickly discover the solution to their inquiry online, a lot of customers will give up on their purchase. They could have looked through your website for the solution and failed.

Upon visiting your Contact Us page, they could have discovered that sending an email is the only way to receive a response, with a maximum of five working days. Alternatively, they could need to contact customer support, but the hours are too tight, or they might just not want to because it's not how they primarily communicate.

1. Implement a feedback management system. You need customer input to be successful. You can maintain relationships with your current clientele and continuously improve your offerings to cater to the demands of potential clients by putting in place a feedback management system that facilitates the tracking and analysis of consumer pain points.

2. Optimize customer journeys: The first step towards removing obstacles and providing individualized customer journeys is determining if the existing solutions being given meet the main pain points of the consumer. You can also test whether the route map is effective for your clients by going through the

procedure yourself and looking for any unforeseen delays. For a more comprehensive approach, you could even choose to enlist the help of experts from other teams.

3. List typical customer complaints: It's vital for any firm to list the most prevalent complaints from customers. You may respond to common questions from your clients by using your knowledge base, self-service portals, or FAQ sites. This raises customer happiness and assists your support personnel in identifying, prioritizing, and resolving urgent pain areas.

4. Automate internal procedures: In order to cut expenses and raise overall productivity, internal procedures must be streamlined. To guarantee that certain issues are forwarded to the appropriate departments and cut down on client wait times, you can implement help desk software.

You can decide to move to an omnichannel platform that offers a more adaptable and comprehensive method of communicating with customers. This means that you might provide a variety of client communication channels, including chatbots, live chat, WhatsApp, calls, contact form forms, and emails, to accommodate a wide range of preferences. Because chatbots are always available, you can now assist clients with any urgent queries they may have at any time.

Making sure your clients realize that you address this pain point is essential after that. Information regarding your company's communication choices and availability should be included in your marketing materials.

Chapter 9: Contentment and loyalty of customers

Before being loyal to a firm, customers must be satisfied with the products it sells. For them to succeed, their clients must be content. So what is the relationship between customer satisfaction and loyalty?

Moreover, how can you gauge success if you can only do one? What criteria are used to gauge client satisfaction? How is client loyalty measured?

It's typically a sign of satisfaction when customers choose to return to your physical business or shop online. However, consumer loyalty is not the same as customer happiness or contentment.

Customers that are happy with your services have the ability and motivation to stick with you and refer you to additional business. Thus, monitoring client contentment and comprehending the connection between retention and satisfaction are critical for every e-commerce company. Considering that dissatisfied clients would definitely decide not to come back.

Customer satisfaction: what is it?

A measure of a customer's level of enjoyment when interacting with and/or making purchases from a business is called customer satisfaction (CSAT). It assesses if your offerings satisfy consumer expectations and how well customers perceive your entire customer experience (CX) and goods.

High customer satisfaction rates translate into successful businesses with lots of recurring revenue from devoted patrons.

Concurrently, a company experiencing dissatisfied clients may observe a high rate of product returns, numerous refund requests, and a general decline in sales.

You must use surveys and get responses from your consumers in order to gauge client satisfaction.

Since the customer experience is the main focus of customer satisfaction, it considers a number of factors.

These factors consist of:

- The accessibility of products
- The purchase procedure
- The encounter after the purchase
- The promptness, friendliness, and helpfulness of your customer service representatives

What makes a satisfied consumer important?

1. Happy consumers may become repeat customers

When consumers are pleased with both a brand's offerings and their interactions with the brand, they are more likely to visit that store again in the future.

Making consumers happy starts with providing them with excellent items. On the other hand, poor customer service damages your brand and raises attrition.

A customer's interactions with your brand can take place via:

1. Making a transaction in person or online

2. Sending inquiries or information requests to customer service

3. Returning a merchandise item

4. Product returns

5. The experience following a transaction.

2) Satisfied clients may assist you in identifying your advantages.

You can determine where your company succeeds and where it falls short by tracking client satisfaction.

Maintaining your standard of excellence is made easier by gathering input through customer satisfaction surveys. Additionally, it guarantees that you are aware of your areas of weakness so that you may strengthen them.

3) Happy clients can recommend you with ease

Getting recommendations is the first step towards achieving customer happiness, which is one of its main advantages.

One excellent and affordable strategy for gaining new clients is through referral marketing. Furthermore, compared to new clients who have never done business with you or who have received a recommendation to test your items, the recommendations are made by pleased and devoted consumers, who are less doubtful of your company.

Referrals originate from happy and devoted clients, so you can bet that they will trust you right away and have less doubts about your company. In comparison, new customers are those who have never purchased from you or received a referral to try one of your items.

4) Reduced churn

It is quite possible that you have come to the realization that contented consumers are less inclined to churn, or defect to a rival brand. To prevent clients from leaving and to have devoted supporters of your company, it is ideal to guarantee steady and continuous customer happiness. Additionally helpful in lowering attrition are tailored experiences and customer interaction tactics.

5. Satisfied clients may increase brand loyalty

Enhanced client loyalty to your brand is an additional advantage of achieving customer happiness.

This materializes in favorable product evaluations and word-of-mouth. Furthermore, it may manifest as recommendations.

How to design a customer satisfaction survey for e-commerce:

It's time to examine the procedures you have to take in order to make an e-commerce client satisfaction survey. It is important to emphasize now, rather than later, that you shouldn't construct a survey in the first place if you don't intend to take action to resolve consumers' problems and unhappiness based on the survey results.

It takes a lot of effort and time to create a survey, get clients to answer, gather data, and analyze the findings.

You must do the following actions in order to generate your e-commerce satisfaction survey:

1. Establish your objectives.

Identifying your goals for customer satisfaction is the first step towards developing an effective survey. What are you hoping to accomplish with this survey?

Are consumers happy with their entire shopping experience at your store?

Have you just added a new product line or partner that you'd want to know what your consumers think of?

You must take each of these objectives into account in this stage. The objective you select here will determine the form of your survey questions.

2. Make a strategy

Once you've written down your objectives, it's time to develop a strategy to get you there. Once your results are in, you may go back and review this area to make note of the things you need to improve on and the things you need to fix.

3. Select the type of survey.

Three key criteria should be taken into account when assessing customer happiness. They are as follows:

1. customer satisfaction rating (CSAT)

2. The Net Promoter Index (NPI)

3. A measure of customer effort (CES)

Selecting which of these survey formats and measures for customer satisfaction to utilize is up to you. This question has no right or incorrect response. All of them work well, despite minor variations.

4. Form a series of inquiries

Here's the moment to put your survey questions on paper. For the many components of satisfaction that you want to gauge, you may create recurrent questions.

Some examples of inquiries on customer satisfaction include:

1. How pleased are you with [product name/product line]?

2. In the U.S, we've started employing a new delivery service. Tell us how satisfied you are with this new service, please.

Extended questionnaires including unrestricted inquiry options can also be designed to allow clients to clarify issues or provide recommendations.

Does [brand name] need to make any improvements, in your opinion? Please offer your suggestions below.

Keep in mind that a survey should not have too many questions. The likelihood of a client responding to a survey increases with its length.

5. Have your survey's trigger created.

Include triggers in your survey design as part of your planning process. A survey question is triggered by a customer's single action in an automation called a trigger.

Five online purchases or the completion of one by a consumer can serve as triggers. It could also occur when a consumer decides to exchange an item for a refund, return an item, or take another action.

Quarterly or yearly surveys are a decision made by certain brands.

Following a customer's purchase, for instance, a lot of businesses send out surveys, such as this one, with only one question:

Please give [brand name] a rating based on your most recent experience. OR Kindly provide a rating for your recent online shopping experience at [brand name]. Ten are really happy, and one is quite unhappy.

6. Examine the findings

After the completion of your satisfaction survey, it's time to review the data and assess the performance of your online business.

7. Modify and try again

It's time to assess your procedure and outcomes after finishing your e-commerce company's client satisfaction survey and receiving feedback.

Next, take what you've learned from this experience and use it to automate future surveys and queries about client satisfaction.

This might involve developing fresh triggers, extending survey questions, and implementing some or all of the suggestions you get from those questionnaires.

How to improve online shopping experience for customers

1. Offer first-rate client assistance

An attentive and helpful customer support staff is the most important tool you can utilize to improve client happiness and retention.

It's a costly undertaking, even if clients might expect you to provide 24/7 help. Prominent B2B companies such as PayPal, Stripe, Ubersuggest, and Freepik do not offer round-the-clock customer service. Their chatbot provides information about when they are and are not available. Customers are also told that they will hear back from them in less than 48 hours. In most cases, the answer comes faster. In order to satisfy consumers, these companies provide themselves a 48-hour cushion so that their staff may answer ahead of schedule.

The group that interacts with customers is your customer support team. Make sure your staff is excellent, understanding, and quick to answer to consumers, whether they contact you by email, chat, or phone.

2. Inform clients of updates

Make sure to inform them about any site outages, fresh upgrades, new merchandise, etc. Don't go overboard though!

Although clients like participating in surveys, avoid bombarding them. If not, you'll witness the second unfavorable aspect of excessive client communication.

3. Provide incentives for consumers to participate in surveys: Offering rewards for survey participation is a terrific method to encourage people to take part. You

may provide incentives by utilizing a client loyalty and rewards program.

Financial incentives are inappropriate; that would be considered bribery!

When consumers finish a monthly survey, you may give them points. Customers who finish one or more surveys can receive points and a badge as part of a monthly survey challenge you can establish using Gameball.

The longer the survey, the better the reward becomes as well. It appears from this that a customer can get 10 or 50 points for responding to a single survey item. Users can win incentives worth $10 or 100–200 points by completing a 10-minute survey in the interim.

How frequently should the level of customer satisfaction be assessed? Clearly, there isn't a universal answer to this query. Every company is different. Small companies are interested in learning more about their consumers' opinions, but they also don't want to come across as intrusive. Larger companies, on the other hand, don't want to abuse their clients' confidence by inundating them with emails on their happiness.

Here are some suggestions on when to inquire about a customer's level of satisfaction:

1. Introducing a fresh campaign

2. Following the introduction of a new product line

3. Following the holidays is an excellent opportunity to inquire about the client experience and how you can make it better because websites are often busy at this time.

4. Make a request following a predetermined number of transactions or significant spending (build an automatic email that is sent out once a consumer spends a predetermined amount or after they finish 10 or 20 purchases).

How to understand your customer behavior

Chapter 10:Tools for Understanding Consumer Buying Patterns

1. Surveys for market research: Qualtrics and SurveyMonkey are two tools that make it easier to create surveys that collect data on customer motives, preferences, and buying patterns.

2. Customer Relationship Management (CRM): HubSpot and Salesforce are two platforms that assist in tracking and managing customer interactions by offering information on past purchases, preferences, and purchasing habits.

3. Consumer Behavior Analytics Tools: Programs such as Adobe Analytics, Mixpanel, or Google Analytics provide information about online user behavior and may be used to better understand how customers use websites and make decisions about what to buy.

4. E-commerce analytics: Sites such as Magento Analytics or Shopify Analytics provide particular

information on online purchasing patterns in e-commerce settings.

5. Social Media Analytics: Programs like BuzzSumo and Facebook Insights examine user behavior, attitudes, and trends on social media sites.

6. Tableau: Data Visualization: Create interactive graphics by importing customer data gathered from several sources. Examine trends and associations in the data to comprehend consumer purchasing patterns.

7. Consumer Panels and Focus Groups: Conventional techniques entail assembling consumer groups for focus groups (FocusVision, UserTesting) or involving consumer panels specifically (Nielsen Consumer Panel) in order to ascertain preferences and purchasing patterns.

8. Behavioral Economics Tools: These resources, like BEworks, use elements of economics and psychology to comprehend how decisions are made.

Here's how to utilize these tools to comprehend customer purchasing patterns step-by-step:

1. Google Analytics:

First Step: Activate Google Analytics: After registering, add the tracking code to your website.

Step 2: Go to the Audience Section and look into the location, age, gender, and interests of the people that are visiting your website.

Step 3: Review Behavior Flow: Examine the Behavior Flow section to learn how visitors move throughout your website.

Step 4: Establish Objectives and Monitor E-Commerce: Establish objectives like purchases and sign-ups. If appropriate, enable tracking for online purchases.

2. Facebook Insights:

Step 1: Go to Access Page Insights. Navigate to your Facebook page and select Insights.

Step 2: Examine Demographics: Examine your page followers' demographics and engagement data.

Step 3: Investigate Post Performance: Examine the effectiveness of various post formats and content kinds to gauge the preferences of your audience.

3. SurveyMonkey:
Step 1: Establish a Survey Create a survey that focuses on the inclinations, purchasing patterns, or satisfaction levels of your target audience.

Step 2: Distribute the Survey: Send out the survey link by email, post it on social media, or include it into your website.

Step 3: Examine Reactions: Gather feedback and utilize SurveyMonkey's analytical capabilities to spot trends and patterns.

4. Salesforce:

Step 1: Customer Profiling: Build thorough customer profiles using Salesforce CRM in conjunction with purchases.

Step 2: Analyze Sales Data: Monitor client contacts throughout the sales cycle and examine the behaviors that result in transactions.

5. Google Trends:

Step 1: Look Into Search Patterns To track search interest over time, enter keywords associated with your business or line of products.

Step Two: Examine Trend Patterns Note any seasonal patterns or shifts in the interests of your customers.

6. Tableau:

Step 1: import customer data. Gather and import customer information into Tableau from several sources.

Step 2: Produce Interactive Visualizations: Construct interactive visualizations to examine trends and connections in the data.

7. Focus groups and survey panels:

Step 1: Arrange Talks: To obtain qualitative insights, arrange consumer panels or focus groups.

Step 2: Hold Meetings Utilize remote session platforms such as FocusVision or UserTesting to gather feedback.

Others consist of;

1. Live Chat: Real-time Human to Human Communication. One tool that helps organizations and customers communicate with one another is live chat. It facilitates faster connection and lets companies get visitor data. The experience of live chatting is one-on-one. Through a real-time interaction, it enables you to delve into your customers' thinking. For customers who are uncomfortable speaking over the phone or in person, it's a fantastic substitute.

To provide a hand, use the Live Visitors List.

With this function, you may get a live summary of every visitor to your website. To initiate a conversation, you can pick certain clients.

For instance: A visitor is now on the page where the shipping charges are displayed. It can be their first time purchasing something from overseas via the internet. The visitor could feel uncertain about placing an order with you as a result.

This is an excellent time to intervene and provide assistance.

Receive alerts when a user becomes "stuck" on a certain page: If you have little traffic, the Live Visitor List Works nicely. Alternatively, when you are pursuing customers that want to purchase pricey goods.

In other circumstances, you can build a basic chatbot to automate the selection procedure and respond to specific client actions. When a visitor has been looking at a page for some time, it will notify you. This might be any page, or it could be a particular page. That is dependent upon your objectives.

For example, spending many minutes on a single page may indicate that the visitor is really engaged in the purchasing process. They may examine your proposal and perhaps contrast it with those of the rivals. Thus, assist them and show that you are a proactive customer service provider.

Utilize the Viewed Pages feature to monitor your visitor's path:

There are impulsive customers. They purchase without thinking. Because they are unsure of what they will ultimately purchase, they frequently don't know what they desire. Alternatively, they may be searching for a gift without having a specific notion in mind.

For example: These clients' purchasing experiences might be quite disorganized. They frequently quickly and haphazardly flip between the pages. You may track the movements of these purchasers and view every page they have visited by using Viewed Pages. Engage in conversation with a visitor you see who has a lot of browsing history. You might be able to advise them on what to buy.

2. Chatbots: Real-time robot-human communication
Statistics from chatbots show that personalized and customized automated messages perform better than generic ones.

Chatbots never get bored and are quick. They may provide 24/7 assistance to any number of clients. They track, communicate, gather, and store information about consumer behavior that you may then evaluate and utilize for marketing or segmentation.

Step 1: To engage with visitors to your website, add a chat plugin.
Step 2: Develop unique chatbots that respond to queries and solicit input.

Step 3: Increase revenue and monitor the benefits of chatbots for your company.

Conclusion

Knowing your clients' wants and the reasons behind them is the key to understanding them, much as when you solve a problem. However, you must appeal to both their emotions and intellect if you want to win them over. Start by employing data and insights to delve deeply into their preferences and actions. That is comprehension. Then, go above and beyond simple transactions and give them a genuine sense of worth and understanding. That is aimed at their feelings and ideas. The crucial point is that providing for them matters more than just what you sell. It's all about establishing mutual trust and understanding. It is the source of devoted clientele. Loyalty blooms when you deliver genuine attention and value on a regular basis. Having supporters who have faith in your business is just as important as having consumers. Therefore, you're creating a unique bond between your business and your clients when you comprehend, target, and appeal to their preferences and feelings. They remain because it seems like they're becoming a part of their tale. Being a dependable friend they can rely on is more important than providing a goods or service.

.

www.ingramcontent.com/pod-product-compliance
Lightning Source LLC
Chambersburg PA
CBHW062322290526
45794CB00005B/1864

* 9 7 9 8 8 7 3 3 5 9 4 8 6 *